A LETTER A WEEK

Your guide to writing and mailing 52 handwritten letters during the year

Julie Merrick

Julie Merrick
P.O. Box 11414
Olympia, WA 98508

Ordering Information:
Quantity sales: Special discounts are available on quantity purchases by corporations, associations, and others. For details, contact the address above.

The publisher is not responsible for websites (or their content) that are not owned by the publisher.

Cover design by Latham Floyde
Edited by Kanoe Namahoe
Photography by Jeffrey Dransfeldt

A Letter A Week Journal, Julie Merrick. —1st ed.
ISBN 987-0-578-31207-1

This journal belongs to:

_____

Please, do the right thing and call

_____

if found.

*Dedicated to my mother, who introduced me
to the joy of handwritten letters.*

Introduction

Thank you for opening this journal! You are about to embark on a yearlong journey of writing 52 handwritten letters. Whether you write letters regularly, or haven't written a letter in years, you will soon be writing and mailing one letter each week.

"I can't write 52 letters!"

Yes, you can. Even better, along the way, you'll find that you enjoy the process.

This is because writing by hand slows you down, it helps you pause. It forces you to be present, to be in a space where your hand is holding a pen and letting your words — your heart, your thoughts — flow onto paper. Handwriting stirs the waters of your creative soul and lets you reflect and share yourself with others.

Don't worry if it feels awkward at first. That's normal. Take your time and let yourself settle into the process. Get a pen that feels good in your hand. Pull out your note cards or stationery. Brew a cup of coffee (or tea), and sit down at your kitchen table or cozy up on the couch. Get comfortable and let your mind relax.

Enjoy yourself! Don't let this become a chore. You can write a few sentences or several pages. You can write to people you know personally, or someone you have never met. It's all up to you. Just be creative and have fun!

The great thing about this journal is it doesn't matter if you complete it in one month, one year, or more. I just hope you take time to slow down, be intentional in reaching out to others, and connect through letters.

I'm rooting for you! And if you ever want to give up or have any questions, please email me at julie@aletteraweek.com or write to me at P.O. Box 11414, Olympia, WA 98508, and I will do my best to help and encourage you to write and send a letter a week.

Let's get started!

Julie

How to Use This Journal

"*Julie, why do I need to keep a log of the letters I write? Doesn't that turn this into a chore?*"

Not at all!

You're not keeping a food log. You're creating a keepsake. This journal will be a bank of memories that you can revisit time and again. Who doesn't want that?

Logging your letters is easy. Every time you send a letter, mark in your journal to whom it was written, where it was sent, for what occasion, and any other pertinent information you want to remember. If you are a big stationery fan like me, include the type of card you sent ("sunset card", blank or "Thinking of you" card, red). This way, if you write to that person again, you'll know which card you sent them. There are 52 entries for logging your correspondence.

Throughout the journal, you will find tips and ideas to help you keep writing. At the end of the journal, there are more pages for creating a master list of everyone you write, tracking birthdays and special occasions, and planning future letters. There are also letter-writing resources and a list of places to purchase cards and stationery.

Keep this journal near your desk or bedside, so that you'll be sure to open it weekly. Think about a day and time you want to do this weekly and put a reminder on your phone.

And that's it! Are you ready? Go write your first letter or keep reading.

ABOUT THAT WORD "LETTER"

I laughed recently as I reread Margaret Shepard's *The Art of the Handwritten Note*. In it, she has a list of "dont's," such as not sending a letter written on notebook paper with holes punched in it, as "that's like going out dressed in only your underpants."

I say, write on whatever you want—greeting card, note-card, postcard, or pretty stationery.

Or a banana leaf. A friend of mine received a birthday gift from her sister in Hawaii. The card? A banana leaf with birthday wishes scribbled on it with a Sharpie. "It was the coolest, most creative card I've ever received," she told me.

Whatever you do, make it your own. What's most important is you taking the time to handwrite your thoughts, opinions, wishes, and more to another person.

Your turn

Place a Post-it® Note by the remote control so you can write a letter instead of watching TV (or write during commercials, as I do).

Family First

S tumped on who to write first? Start with a family member—your grandparents, your mother, your father, a favorite aunt or uncle, or another relative.

"Family? What would I write?"

There's a lot to say! Say thank you to the uncle who taught you how to fish. Reminisce with your cousins about past Christmas holidays and White Elephant gift exchanges. Trade recipes with the niece who just got married and is cooking for her new husband. The possibilities are endless!

Don't overthink it. Have fun and enjoy the stroll down your memory lane.

Stamps

At the time of this publication, January 2022, the price of a First-Class Mail® Forever® letter stamp is $0.58 and $0.40 for a postcard (when in doubt, visit the USPS website to check). It will cost you $30.16 to send 52 letters—less if you mail postcards.

And you don't have to mail all of your letters! Put one on a neighbor's porch or under a coworker's coffee cup. Hand one directly to your favorite barista.

Your Turn

It's easy to purchase stamps online. But why not get to know your local post office employees and purchase from them directly?

And did you know, many major grocery store chains sell stamps? Put stamps on your grocery list and pick them up on your next visit.

Stationery

Gather your supplies — paper or cards, envelopes, a pen, and a stamp. My friend stores her writing supplies in a pretty basket near her desk. It's easy to grab and to move about the house if she wants to write in a different room.

Do you need expensive stationery and cards? Of course not. But is it fun to shop online for cards and other pretty writing tools? Of course, it is! Here are some suggestions:

Check Google: What doesn't Google know? (That's another book for another time.) Do a Google search for "stationery stores near me." Try supporting small local businesses before buying from big retailers like Target. You might be surprised by what you find.

The Dollar Store: Check out dollar stores ($1.25 now?) in your area. Many have greeting cards and packages of two cards for a dollar. Pick up a pack of blank photo note cards to have on hand for different occasions.

Etsy: Etsy.com has beautiful cards and stationery. Get a set of personalized note cards for a friend. Buy yourself a set of handmade, hand-stamped stationery. Need a gift for a young person? Etsy's stationery grab bags — with pretty paper, cards, stickers, and more — make a fun surprise. Bonus: When you buy from Etsy, you support people making their own products.

Are you a DIY diva? Pull out the stamps, stickers, and pens, and craft your own personalized cards and stationery. Make it as elaborate or simple as you want. Once you write on a blank piece of paper, it becomes a one-of-a-kind, special letter from you.

Travel much? Keep a small pouch or Ziploc bag with stationery, a pen, and stamps in your car or travel bag. Or look for cards at car washes and convenience stores; many now carry postcards and greeting cards. As you send more letters, you will notice all the places that sell cards. Just wait.

Need more ideas? Check out page 91 for a list of my favorite places to purchase stationery online.

STATIONERY STORES

I love finding new stationery. One of the first things I do when visiting a new locale is check out its stationery stores. I have found some of the most beautiful papers, cards, and writing instruments in these places. Many times, these are small, family-owned businesses and the owners are just as passionate as I am about paper and writing. These visits are a fun way to get to know a new town and add something to my paper collection.

Your Turn

Think of your favorite pen. (Currently, mine is the Dr. Grip gel pen by Pilot.) Grab a few more—for your purse, briefcase, gym bag, car—to have on hand when you want to write a letter.

You Are Going to Make Mistakes

You are going to spell words wrong. Or write the wrong word and have to scratch it out and start over. (Okay, some of you will use correction tape or—if you're older—the correction fluid.) You are going to omit a letter in a word or a word in a sentence.

You are going to have a pen leak or run out of ink while writing. You are going to judge your handwriting.

You will think of something you should have—or should *not* have—said after mailing the letter. You are going to forget to finish the letter and yet still mail it. You are going to forget the zip code—or the stamp—on the envelope.

Stop.

You're not being graded on your letters. You're not in a competition. You're not going to lose a friend, family member, or colleague over any of these mistakes. I've done all of these— multiple times—and I keep writing letters.

YOUR HANDWRITING IS UNIQUELY YOUR OWN.

Your handwriting captures your personality. Do not apologize for it in your letters. People will appreciate the letter. And your handwriting is part of what makes the letter so special.

Speak Up!

You are thinking about who to write to, but you don't have their address. Awkward, I know.

So try online first. Google is our friend. Many people and businesses have their mailing addresses on their websites. (Remember, there is a difference between someone's physical address—where they live—versus their mailing address, where they receive their mail.)

But if that doesn't work, ask for it. **There is nothing wrong with asking for someone's mailing address.**

Know that you do not have to send something the day you get the person's address. That is where the element of surprise comes in. It may be a few days, weeks, or months before he or she receives your note.

Your Turn

Go ask for someone's address and fill it in the journal for a future letter on page 84.

Who Else Can You Write?

If you have an extended family and a lot of friends then you have plenty of people to write to.

But try and mix it up! Start writing to, what I like to call " People I appreciate and want to thank." You may not know these people personally. Remember, it is not about you. You are sending cheer and appreciation to someone else. Take a look at this list and start getting addresses, or hand letters to them personally:

- accountant or tax preparer
- acquaintances
- attorneys
- clergy
- clients
- coaches (especially those in volunteer or public school settings)
- co-workers
- customers
- educators (don't forget paraprofessionals, administrators, office, and other support staff)
- local and national politicians
- local charities
- local Fire and Police Departments
- neighbors

- organizations and clubs doing positive things for your community and the world
- postal workers
- vendors with whom you do business with regularly
- volunteer organizations you support

Your turn

Think of people and places you give your time and money to daily, weekly, monthly, occasionally (take a look at your bank statement): gas stations, grocery stores, coffee shops, restaurants, doctor's offices, healthcare providers, optometrist, dentist, pharmacist, blood bank, hair salon, nail salon, spa, or a dry cleaner.

What to Write?

It's YOUR letter. Write whatever you want! Think simple. It should not take long, or be burdensome.

Think of the recipient. Where might they be when they receive your letter? At home, maybe sipping wine and relaxing? Or maybe at their desk at work. If it's at work, then you probably do not want to pen a four-page, front and back letter.

Write as if you are talking to the person. Treat it like a conversation. Share what's happening in your life. Did you start a new diet or exercise regime? Have you visited a cool new restaurant or tried a new recipe that he or she would like? Are you going on vacation soon? What's new with the kids? These are all good places to start.

Do you share a special memory with them? Talk about that. It's always pleasurable to recall memories of a good time, especially if you haven't thought about it in years.

What about sharing a dream you have for the future? Could you ask deeper questions for them to ponder, or simply share what you've been up to lately?

Are you a good storyteller? Tell a story in your letter! Write a poem, or even lyrics to a song you enjoy.

Do you want to write about politics or religion? Go for it! You can also tell a joke, share a quote you like, or share how you felt after reading a book or article.

Some letters will be surface-level. That's fine—it's all up to you. Letters do not have to be a "tell-all" about your entire life. You will find, as you exchange letters with someone, that your letters cover all kinds of topics.

Some of the most delightful letters I've received have been a postcard with one or two sentences, or a funny greeting card with just the sender's name in ink. Remember, this is your letter, so write what feels satisfying to you.

A NOTE ABOUT PEN PALS

This project is for you to write 52 letters, not to become a pen pal. You do not have to write back to people, although many of you will. However, if you are interested in becoming a pen pal, check out pages 89-90 for links to organizations you may want to join.

Your Turn

Don't forget to put the date at the top of your letter! Someone may read the letter years from now. You will want them to know when it was written.

When and Where to Write

Wherever — and whenever — you can write, write! Some of you will want peace and quietness; others will prefer a bustling coffee shop. I often sit on the couch with a book on top of a pillow to write during commercials when watching television.

Do you taxi kids around? Try dashing off a quick letter while in the carpool line at school or sports practice. Or could you jot down a letter while sitting next to your children as they do their homework? What a great way to model letter writing for them.

Write on a plane. It's always fun to say, "writing to you from 36,000 feet." If there is turbulence, you even have an excuse for the sloppy writing!

Write in bed, in the car, at the beach, at a park, or even your office. Find what works for you.

My roommate from college wrote to me recently about letter writing and said, "Once I sit down and DO IT, it is a very enjoyable thing."

I hope you find that it is too.

FAMILY TIME OUT

Do you and your family do "digital breaks"—ditching phones and devices for a specific length of time? What if everyone sat down and wrote a letter? What a great way to start a family tradition! Please send me a photo if you do.

Your Turn

Set a reminder on your phone to write a letter. When it goes off, turn on your favorite music, and spend 10 minutes writing a letter.

Greeting Cards

According to the Greeting Card Association, the most popular card-sending occasion is a birthday. Other commonly known card categories, in order of popularity:

Sympathy	Get Well
Thank You	New Baby
Wedding	Congratulations
Thinking of You	

Here are the most popular national holidays:

Christmas	Mother's Day
Easter	St. Patrick's Day
Father's Day	Thanksgiving
Halloween	Valentine's Day

Check out the National Day Calendar online to find more holidays. There are national days, weeks, and months for everything. This website is all you need to find a reason to write to someone!

Got a friend who loves cheese? Send them a letter letting them know you are thinking of them on January 20, "National Cheese Day." Go out with the girls on September 22—"National Girls'

Night" — and give them all personalized stationery. Show your contractor that you appreciate his work with a handwritten thank you card on July 14, "National Tape Measure Day." The possibilities are endless!

ENVELOPES

Google "decorative envelopes" or "envelope art", and you'll be inspired by the creative ways people address envelopes. Not artsy? Try adding something unexpected in the envelope like confetti, a gift card, or a drawing you made. Some favorites that a few of my friends always add: a feather, a lottery ticket, or a package of flower seeds.

Postcards

The best thing about postcards is that you don't have to write much and you don't need an envelope. Postcard stamps are cheaper than regular stamps, ($0.40 vs $0.58) and are available all over the world.

Here are some ideas for using postcards:

- Purchase postcards from where you live and send them to friends who used to live near you or have never visited
- Collect postcards when you travel and mail later, sharing a memory about the trip
- Kids love postcards! Pick one up at an airport or souvenir shop when traveling and drop it in the mail to a special niece, nephew or young person
- Buy a box of postcards for a friend then start a fun letter exchange using just a postcard
- Did you know you can mail a photo? Simply print out your photo, (3"x5" or 4"x6") write a short greeting on the left side, put the address on the right, add a stamp and mail. Voila!

Your Turn

Got a museum, hotel, or visitor's center nearby? Take a quick run down there and pick up a few postcards to mail.

More Reasons to Send Letters

Here are additional types of letters to send. You can find cards in several of these categories at stores that sell greeting cards.

Apologies. A simple "I'm sorry" can go a long way.

Baby Shower, Bridal Shower

Children. Put a note, or better yet, a letter in their lunch bag. Try having a special theme for what you will write about in future letters.

Adoption	Graduations
Anniversaries	Job promotion
Congratulations	New baby, New home
Engagement, Wedding	New job, New pet
Good news, Good luck	Retirement

Happy birthday. Also, half-birthdays are a fun twist on the annual milestone. Pick someone's birthday and write down their half-birthday on page 86.

Just because	Sharing a special memory
Just wanted to say hi	Holidays *(see page 15)*
Haven't heard from you in a while	Sympathy

Again, turn to page 84 and jot down a few future letters you plan to send. Or if you need help with what words to say for these different occasions, check out the resources on pages 87-92.

Write It, Mail It, Let It Go

One thing about letter writing is that you must not expect anything in return. There are people to whom I have written and never received an acknowledgment—maybe they never received it or it didn't occur to them to respond. Who says they have to? The only time I would ask is if it included cash or a gift card.

Not everyone cares about receiving a letter and if you are writing to a celebrity or someone famous, then you really must *let it go*. I have written to authors and columnists and it is always a surprise to hear back. For the times when I didn't hear back, I still know I reached out to thank them and to share how their works influenced me.

Think about someone's work you appreciate (celebrity or not) and send them a letter!

I do believe that even if the recipient does not respond to your letter, they will be touched by your thoughtfulness. There is giving and receiving in letter writing, regardless of whether you get a response. Everyone views this differently. The gifts from giving are not in the form of a present that you open (though they could be)—they are personal and internal. I hope you experience many gifts during the year that come from sending these letters.

Get started writing your first letter!

Letter 1

Date sent: _____

To: _____

Birthday	☐	**Hello**	☐	**Sympathy**	☐
Congratulations	☐	**Holiday**	☐	**Thank you**	☐
Get Well	☐	**Remember When**	☐	**Thinking of you**	☐
Other	☐				

Address:

_____

_____

Stationery Used:

_____

_____

Misc. Comments:

_____

_____

Cue the confetti!

You wrote your first letter — congratulations!

There's something very satisfying about sealing the envelope, applying a stamp on it, and dropping it in the mailbox. I often envision the recipient receiving it and smiling as they read.

You are officially on your way!

Do something this week to celebrate your win. Buy a new pen, give yourself a high five, or have a piece of cake!

Letter 2

Date sent: _____

To: _____

Birthday	☐	**Hello**	☐	**Sympathy**	☐
Congratulations	☐	**Holiday**	☐	**Thank you**	☐
Get Well	☐	**Remember When**	☐	**Thinking of you**	☐
Other	☐				

Address:

_____

_____

Stationery Used:

_____

_____

Misc. Comments:

_____

_____

Letter 3

Date sent: _____

To: _____

Birthday	☐	**Hello**	☐	**Sympathy**	☐
Congratulations	☐	**Holiday**	☐	**Thank you**	☐
Get Well	☐	**Remember When**	☐	**Thinking of you**	☐
Other	☐				

Address:

_____

_____

Stationery Used:

_____

_____

Misc. Comments:

_____

_____

Letter 4

Date sent: _____

To: _____

Birthday	☐	**Hello**	☐	**Sympathy**	☐
Congratulations	☐	**Holiday**	☐	**Thank you**	☐
Get Well	☐	**Remember When**	☐	**Thinking of you**	☐
Other	☐				

Address:

_____

_____

Stationery Used:

_____

_____

Misc. Comments:

_____

_____

Letter 5

Date sent: _____

To: _____

Birthday	☐	**Hello**	☐	**Sympathy**	☐
Congratulations	☐	**Holiday**	☐	**Thank you**	☐
Get Well	☐	**Remember When**	☐	**Thinking of you**	☐
Other	☐				

Address:

_____

_____

Stationery Used:

_____

_____

Misc. Comments:

_____

_____

Letter 6

Date sent: _____

To: _____

Birthday	☐	**Hello**	☐	**Sympathy**	☐
Congratulations	☐	**Holiday**	☐	**Thank you**	☐
Get Well	☐	**Remember When**	☐	**Thinking of you**	☐
Other	☐				

Address:

_____

_____

Stationery Used:

_____

_____

Misc. Comments:

_____

_____

Letter 7

Date sent: _____

To: _____

Birthday	☐	**Hello**	☐	**Sympathy**	☐
Congratulations	☐	**Holiday**	☐	**Thank you**	☐
Get Well	☐	**Remember When**	☐	**Thinking of you**	☐
Other	☐				

Address:

_____

_____

Stationery Used:

_____

_____

Misc. Comments:

_____

_____

Letter 8

Date sent: _____

To: _____

Birthday	☐	**Hello**	☐	**Sympathy**	☐
Congratulations	☐	**Holiday**	☐	**Thank you**	☐
Get Well	☐	**Remember When**	☐	**Thinking of you**	☐
Other	☐				

Address:

_____

_____

Stationery Used:

_____

_____

Misc. Comments:

_____

_____

Use Numbers

Try using numbers to punch up your letters.

Write "_____ of 52" on your envelopes or in your letters to let the recipient know about your goal of writing a letter a week.

How old is your child? Let's say they're 12. Write a letter listing 12 things you love about them or memories you have of them. This is a great exercise for birthdays and anniversaries.

> There's *one* thing special about you …
> These are *three* favorite memories of us …
> *Ten* reasons why I love you …

Letter 9

Date sent: _____

To: _____

Birthday	☐	**Hello**	☐	**Sympathy**	☐
Congratulations	☐	**Holiday**	☐	**Thank you**	☐
Get Well	☐	**Remember When**	☐	**Thinking of you**	☐
Other	☐				

Address:

_____

_____

Stationery Used:

_____

_____

Misc. Comments:

_____

_____

Letter 10

Date sent: _____

To: _____

Birthday ☐	**Hello** ☐	**Sympathy** ☐
Congratulations ☐	**Holiday** ☐	**Thank you** ☐
Get Well ☐	**Remember When** ☐	**Thinking of you** ☐
Other ☐		

Address:

_____

_____

Stationery Used:

_____

_____

Misc. Comments:

_____

_____

Letter 11

Date sent: _____

To: _____

Birthday	☐	**Hello**	☐	**Sympathy**	☐
Congratulations	☐	**Holiday**	☐	**Thank you**	☐
Get Well	☐	**Remember When**	☐	**Thinking of you**	☐
Other	☐				

Address:

_____

_____

Stationery Used:

_____

_____

Misc. Comments:

_____

_____

Letter 12

Date sent: _____

To: _____

Birthday ☐	**Hello** ☐	**Sympathy** ☐
Congratulations ☐	**Holiday** ☐	**Thank you** ☐
Get Well ☐	**Remember When** ☐	**Thinking of you** ☐
Other ☐		

Address:

_____

_____

Stationery Used:

_____

_____

Misc. Comments:

_____

_____

Letter 13

Date sent: _____

To: _____

Birthday ☐	Hello ☐	Sympathy ☐
Congratulations ☐	Holiday ☐	Thank you ☐
Get Well ☐	Remember When ☐	Thinking of you ☐
Other ☐		

Address:

_____

_____

Stationery Used:

_____

_____

Misc. Comments:

_____

_____

Letter 14

Date sent: _____

To: _____

Birthday	☐	**Hello**	☐	**Sympathy**	☐
Congratulations	☐	**Holiday**	☐	**Thank you**	☐
Get Well	☐	**Remember When**	☐	**Thinking of you**	☐
Other	☐				

Address:

_____

_____

Stationery Used:

_____

_____

Misc. Comments:

_____

_____

Letter 15

Date sent: _____

To: _____

Birthday	☐	**Hello**	☐	**Sympathy**	☐
Congratulations	☐	**Holiday**	☐	**Thank you**	☐
Get Well	☐	**Remember When**	☐	**Thinking of you**	☐
Other	☐				

Address:

_____

_____

Stationery Used:

_____

_____

Misc. Comments:

_____

_____

Letter 16

Date sent: _____

To: _____

Birthday ☐	**Hello** ☐	**Sympathy** ☐
Congratulations ☐	**Holiday** ☐	**Thank you** ☐
Get Well ☐	**Remember When** ☐	**Thinking of you** ☐
Other ☐		

Address:

_____

_____

Stationery Used:

_____

_____

Misc. Comments:

_____

_____

Four months of writing letters!

How about writing to parents for the next few months?

Parenting is tough work (especially during a pandemic!). Send letters to a parent (or parents) to encourage them, thank them, or to set up a coffee date away from the kids.

Know a parent that is always there for your child?

Is there a parent who needs to be reminded they are doing a great job?

Can you think of a parent you admire?

Did a parent help you with something?

Write a list of who will receive these future letters on page 84.

Letter 17

Date sent: _____

To: _____

Birthday ☐	Hello ☐	Sympathy ☐
Congratulations ☐	Holiday ☐	Thank you ☐
Get Well ☐	Remember When ☐	Thinking of you ☐
Other ☐		

Address:

_____

_____

Stationery Used:

_____

_____

Misc. Comments:

_____

_____

Letter 18

Date sent: _____

To: _____

Birthday	☐	**Hello**	☐	**Sympathy**	☐
Congratulations	☐	**Holiday**	☐	**Thank you**	☐
Get Well	☐	**Remember When**	☐	**Thinking of you**	☐
Other	☐				

Address:

_____

_____

Stationery Used:

_____

_____

Misc. Comments:

_____

_____

Letter 19

Date sent: _____

To: _____

Birthday	☐	**Hello**	☐	**Sympathy**	☐
Congratulations	☐	**Holiday**	☐	**Thank you**	☐
Get Well	☐	**Remember When**	☐	**Thinking of you**	☐
Other	☐				

Address:

_____

_____

Stationery Used:

_____

_____

Misc. Comments:

_____

_____

Letter 20

Date sent: _____

To: _____

Birthday	☐	**Hello**	☐	**Sympathy**	☐
Congratulations	☐	**Holiday**	☐	**Thank you**	☐
Get Well	☐	**Remember When**	☐	**Thinking of you**	☐
Other	☐				

Address:

_____

_____

Stationery Used:

_____

_____

Misc. Comments:

_____

_____

Letter 21

Date sent: _____

To: _____

Birthday ☐   Hello ☐   Sympathy ☐

Congratulations ☐ Holiday ☐   Thank you ☐

Get Well ☐   Remember When ☐   Thinking of you ☐

Other ☐

Address:

_____

_____

Stationery Used:

_____

_____

Misc. Comments:

_____

_____

Letter 22

Date sent: _____

To: _____

Birthday	☐	**Hello**	☐	**Sympathy**	☐
Congratulations	☐	**Holiday**	☐	**Thank you**	☐
Get Well	☐	**Remember When**	☐	**Thinking of you**	☐
Other	☐				

Address:

_____

_____

Stationery Used:

_____

_____

Misc. Comments:

_____

_____

Strawberry
Letter 23

(I had to! Make this one a love letter. Google it if you don't know this classic 70's hit!)

Date sent: _____

To: _____

Birthday	☐	**Hello**	☐	**Sympathy**	☐
Congratulations	☐	**Holiday**	☐	**Thank you**	☐
Get Well	☐	**Remember When**	☐	**Thinking of you**	☐
Other	☐				

Address:

_____

_____

Stationery Used:

_____

_____

Misc. Comments:

_____

_____

Letter 24

Date sent: _____

To: _____

Birthday	☐	**Hello**	☐	**Sympathy**	☐
Congratulations	☐	**Holiday**	☐	**Thank you**	☐
Get Well	☐	**Remember When**	☐	**Thinking of you**	☐
Other	☐				

Address:

_____

_____

Stationery Used:

_____

_____

Misc. Comments:

_____

_____

Letter 25

Date sent: _____

To: _____

Birthday	☐	**Hello**	☐	**Sympathy**	☐
Congratulations	☐	**Holiday**	☐	**Thank you**	☐
Get Well	☐	**Remember When**	☐	**Thinking of you**	☐
Other	☐				

Address:

_____

_____

Stationery Used:

_____

_____

Misc. Comments:

_____

_____

Letter 26

Date sent: _____

To: _____

Birthday	☐	**Hello**	☐	**Sympathy**	☐
Congratulations	☐	**Holiday**	☐	**Thank you**	☐
Get Well	☐	**Remember When**	☐	**Thinking of you**	☐
Other	☐				

Address:

_____

_____

Stationery Used:

_____

_____

Misc. Comments:

_____

_____

Halfway Home

Congratulations on writing for six months! Look back to see your progress, who you've connected with, and who you can write to again.

Don't stop now! You've got the hang of this. Keep writing and sending letters!

Letter 27

Date sent: _____

To: _____

Birthday	☐	**Hello**	☐	**Sympathy**	☐
Congratulations	☐	**Holiday**	☐	**Thank you**	☐
Get Well	☐	**Remember When**	☐	**Thinking of you**	☐
Other	☐				

Address:

_____

_____

Stationery Used:

_____

_____

Misc. Comments:

_____

_____

Letter 28

Date sent: _____

To: _____

Birthday	☐	Hello	☐	Sympathy	☐
Congratulations	☐	Holiday	☐	Thank you	☐
Get Well	☐	Remember When	☐	Thinking of you	☐
Other	☐				

Address:

_____

_____

Stationery Used:

_____

_____

Misc. Comments:

_____

_____

Letter 29

Date sent: _____

To: _____

Birthday	☐	Hello	☐	Sympathy	☐
Congratulations	☐	Holiday	☐	Thank you	☐
Get Well	☐	Remember When	☐	Thinking of you	☐
Other	☐				

Address:

_____

_____

Stationery Used:

_____

_____

Misc. Comments:

_____

_____

Letter 30

Date sent: _____

To: _____

Birthday	☐	Hello	☐	Sympathy	☐
Congratulations	☐	Holiday	☐	Thank you	☐
Get Well	☐	Remember When	☐	Thinking of you	☐
Other	☐				

Address:

_____

_____

Stationery Used:

_____

_____

Misc. Comments:

_____

_____

Letter 31

Date sent: _____

To: _____

Birthday	☐	**Hello**	☐	**Sympathy**	☐
Congratulations	☐	**Holiday**	☐	**Thank you**	☐
Get Well	☐	**Remember When**	☐	**Thinking of you**	☐
Other	☐				

Address:

_____

_____

Stationery Used:

_____

_____

Misc. Comments:

_____

_____

Letter 32

Date sent: _____

To: _____

Birthday	☐	**Hello**	☐	**Sympathy**	☐
Congratulations	☐	**Holiday**	☐	**Thank you**	☐
Get Well	☐	**Remember When**	☐	**Thinking of you**	☐
Other	☐				

Address:

_____

_____

Stationery Used:

_____

_____

Misc. Comments:

_____

_____

Tell Me Who!

Need more inspiration on who to write? Answer these questions to shake the cobwebs loose:

Who makes you smile? _____

Who makes you laugh? _____

Who makes great meals? _____

Who is fun to go out and do
things with? _____

Who is always there for you? _____

Who can you confide in? _____

Who inspires you? _____

Who do you need to forgive? _____

Who do you take for granted? _____

Who does little things for
you that mean a lot?   _____

Who is loyal?   _____

Who is someone who always
listens to your ideas and
crazy thoughts?   _____

Who is someone who would
never expect a letter in the
mail from you?   _____ _____

There you go. You now have 13 more ideas for who to write.

Letter 33

Date sent: _____

To: _____

Birthday	☐	**Hello**	☐	**Sympathy**	☐
Congratulations	☐	**Holiday**	☐	**Thank you**	☐
Get Well	☐	**Remember When**	☐	**Thinking of you**	☐
Other	☐				

Address:

_____

_____

Stationery Used:

_____

_____

Misc. Comments:

_____

_____

Letter 34

Date sent: _____

To: _____

Birthday	☐	**Hello**	☐	**Sympathy**	☐
Congratulations	☐	**Holiday**	☐	**Thank you**	☐
Get Well	☐	**Remember When**	☐	**Thinking of you**	☐
Other	☐				

Address:

_____

_____

Stationery Used:

_____

_____

Misc. Comments:

_____

_____

Letter 35

Date sent: _____

To: _____

Birthday	☐	**Hello**	☐	**Sympathy**	☐
Congratulations	☐	**Holiday**	☐	**Thank you**	☐
Get Well	☐	**Remember When**	☐	**Thinking of you**	☐
Other	☐				

Address:

_____

_____

Stationery Used:

_____

_____

Misc. Comments:

_____

_____

Letter 36

Date sent: _____

To: _____

Birthday	☐	**Hello**	☐	**Sympathy**	☐
Congratulations	☐	**Holiday**	☐	**Thank you**	☐
Get Well	☐	**Remember When**	☐	**Thinking of you**	☐
Other	☐				

Address:

_____

_____

Stationery Used:

_____

_____

Misc. Comments:

_____

_____

Letter 37

Date sent: _____

To: _____

Birthday	☐	**Hello**	☐	**Sympathy**	☐
Congratulations	☐	**Holiday**	☐	**Thank you**	☐
Get Well	☐	**Remember When**	☐	**Thinking of you**	☐
Other	☐				

Address:

_____

_____

Stationery Used:

_____

_____

Misc. Comments:

_____

_____

Letter 38

Date sent: _____

To: _____

Birthday ☐	Hello ☐	Sympathy ☐
Congratulations ☐	Holiday ☐	Thank you ☐
Get Well ☐	Remember When ☐	Thinking of you ☐
Other ☐		

Address:

_____

_____

Stationery Used:

_____

_____

Misc. Comments:

_____

_____

Letter 39

Date sent: _____

To: _____

Birthday	☐	**Hello**	☐	**Sympathy**	☐
Congratulations	☐	**Holiday**	☐	**Thank you**	☐
Get Well	☐	**Remember When**	☐	**Thinking of you**	☐
Other	☐				

Address:

_____

_____

Stationery Used:

_____

_____

Misc. Comments:

_____

_____

Letter 40

Date sent: _____

To: _____

Birthday	☐	**Hello**	☐	**Sympathy**	☐
Congratulations	☐	**Holiday**	☐	**Thank you**	☐
Get Well	☐	**Remember When**	☐	**Thinking of you**	☐
Other	☐				

Address:

_____

_____

Stationery Used:

_____

_____

Misc. Comments:

_____

_____

Letter 41

Date sent: _____

To: _____

Birthday	☐	**Hello**	☐	**Sympathy**	☐
Congratulations	☐	**Holiday**	☐	**Thank you**	☐
Get Well	☐	**Remember When**	☐	**Thinking of you**	☐
Other	☐				

Address:

_____

_____

Stationery Used:

_____

_____

Misc. Comments:

_____

_____

Letter 42

Date sent: _____

To: _____

Birthday	☐	**Hello**	☐	**Sympathy**	☐
Congratulations	☐	**Holiday**	☐	**Thank you**	☐
Get Well	☐	**Remember When**	☐	**Thinking of you**	☐
Other	☐				

Address:

_____

_____

Stationery Used:

_____

_____

Misc. Comments:

_____

_____

"Thinking of you" letters

Has someone been on your mind lately? That's who you need to write!

Why are you thinking of them? Did you remember something funny, inspiring, or witty they said? Has it been a while since you have seen them? Is there something you've been wanting to say, but haven't? It's time to tell them! Write a letter letting them know you are thinking of them with a sentence or two about why.

What about that someone special who's been running through your thoughts? Jot them a quick letter telling them what you love about them.

Are you concerned about someone? Write a simple letter expressing this. Ask how you can support them.

Need help getting started? Brainstorm about the person. What words come to mind when you think of them? When I think of my friends, here's what pops into my head:

Inspiring, full of love, positive, strong, creative, and respected.

Use one (or a few!) of these words in your letter. Try not to overthink it. Write from the heart and let the words flow onto the page.

10 letters to go!

Letter 43

Date sent: _____

To: _____

Birthday ☐   Hello ☐   Sympathy ☐

Congratulations ☐   Holiday ☐   Thank you ☐

Get Well ☐   Remember When ☐   Thinking of you ☐

Other ☐

Address:

_____

_____

Stationery Used:

_____

_____

Misc. Comments:

_____

_____

Letter 44

Date sent: _____

To: _____

Birthday	☐	**Hello**	☐	**Sympathy**	☐
Congratulations	☐	**Holiday**	☐	**Thank you**	☐
Get Well	☐	**Remember When**	☐	**Thinking of you**	☐
Other	☐				

Address:

_____

_____

Stationery Used:

_____

_____

Misc. Comments:

_____

_____

Letter 45

Date sent: _____

To: _____

Birthday ☐	**Hello** ☐	**Sympathy** ☐
Congratulations ☐	**Holiday** ☐	**Thank you** ☐
Get Well ☐	**Remember When** ☐	**Thinking of you** ☐
Other ☐		

Address:

_____

_____

Stationery Used:

_____

_____

Misc. Comments:

_____

_____

Letter 46

Date sent: _____

To: _____

Birthday ☐	Hello ☐	Sympathy ☐
Congratulations ☐	Holiday ☐	Thank you ☐
Get Well ☐	Remember When ☐	Thinking of you ☐
Other ☐		

Address:

_____

_____

Stationery Used:

_____

_____

Misc. Comments:

_____

_____

Letter 47

Date sent: _____

To: _____

Birthday	☐	**Hello**	☐	**Sympathy**	☐
Congratulations	☐	**Holiday**	☐	**Thank you**	☐
Get Well	☐	**Remember When**	☐	**Thinking of you**	☐
Other	☐				

Address:

_____

_____

Stationery Used:

_____

_____

Misc. Comments:

_____

_____

Letter 48

Date sent: _____

To: _____

Birthday	☐	**Hello**	☐	**Sympathy**	☐
Congratulations	☐	**Holiday**	☐	**Thank you**	☐
Get Well	☐	**Remember When**	☐	**Thinking of you**	☐
Other	☐				

Address:

_____

_____

Stationery Used:

_____

_____

Misc. Comments:

_____

_____

Letter 49

Date sent: _____

To: _____

Birthday	☐	**Hello**	☐	**Sympathy**	☐
Congratulations	☐	**Holiday**	☐	**Thank you**	☐
Get Well	☐	**Remember When**	☐	**Thinking of you**	☐
Other	☐				

Address:

_____

_____

Stationery Used:

_____

_____

Misc. Comments:

_____

_____

Letter 50

Date sent: _____

To: _____

Birthday	☐	Hello	☐	Sympathy	☐
Congratulations	☐	Holiday	☐	Thank you	☐
Get Well	☐	Remember When	☐	Thinking of you	☐
Other	☐				

Address:

_____

_____

Stationery Used:

_____

_____

Misc. Comments:

_____

_____

Date sent: _____

To: _____

Birthday	☐	**Hello**	☐	**Sympathy**	☐
Congratulations	☐	**Holiday**	☐	**Thank you**	☐
Get Well	☐	**Remember When**	☐	**Thinking of you**	☐
Other	☐				

Address:

_____

_____

Stationery Used:

_____

_____

Misc. Comments:

_____

_____

Letter 52

Date sent: _____

To: _____

Birthday	☐	**Hello**	☐	**Sympathy**	☐
Congratulations	☐	**Holiday**	☐	**Thank you**	☐
Get Well	☐	**Remember When**	☐	**Thinking of you**	☐
Other	☐				

Address:

_____

_____

Stationery Used:

_____

_____

Misc. Comments:

_____

_____

Master List of Weekly Letters

1. Lisa ♡
2. Debra ♡
3. Dean ♡
4. Mel ♡
5. Maya ♡
6. Dirinanne ♡
7. Ethan ♡
8. Aunt Betty ♡
9. Sara ♡
10. Lola ♡
11. Carmen ♡
12. Anya ♡
13. Marty ♡
14. _____
15. _____
16. _____
17. _____
18. _____

Master List of Weekly Letters (continued)

19. _____

20. _____

21. _____

22. _____

23. _____

24. _____

25. _____

26. _____

27. _____

28. _____

29. _____

30. _____

31. _____

32. _____

33. _____

34. _____

35. _____

36. _____

37. _____

38. _____

39. _____

Master List of Weekly Letters (continued)

40. _____

41. _____

42. _____

43. _____

44. _____

45. _____

46. _____

47. _____

48. _____

49. _____

50. _____

51. _____

52. _____

Congratulations!
You did it!

_____

(Your name here)

Wrote and sent 52 handwritten letters between

_____and_____

(Dates sent)

Thank you for keeping
handwritten letters alive!

Future Letters to Write

To	For	Sent
_____	_____	☐
_____	_____	☐
_____	_____	☐
_____	_____	☐
_____	_____	☐
_____	_____	☐
_____	_____	☐
_____	_____	☐
_____	_____	☐
_____	_____	☐
_____	_____	☐
_____	_____	☐
_____	_____	☐
_____	_____	☐
_____	_____	☐
_____	_____	☐
_____	_____	☐
_____	_____	☐
_____	_____	☐
_____	_____	☐
_____	_____	☐
_____	_____	☐

Birthday List

Name   Birthday

_____   _____

_____   _____

_____   _____

_____   _____

_____   _____

_____   _____

_____   _____

_____   _____

_____   _____

_____   _____

_____   _____

_____   _____

_____   _____

_____   _____

_____   _____

½ Birthday Date List

Name	Half Birthday Date
_____	_____
_____	_____
_____	_____
_____	_____
_____	_____
_____	_____
_____	_____
_____	_____
_____	_____
_____	_____
_____	_____
_____	_____
_____	_____
_____	_____
_____	_____
_____	_____
_____	_____
_____	_____

My Favorites

DISCLAIMER: I have no affiliation with these companies and receive no compensation, just pure joy of admiring and purchasing their products.

To have this list, (pages 88-92) including even more resources with hyperlinks, so you don't have to type the web addresses, use the QR code below on your phone, or email aletteraweekjournal@gmail.com, and type "website links" in the subject.

Miscellaneous

Celebrity mailing addresses
http://www.fanmail.biz/

Here is a fun page with mind-blowing mail facts!
https://facts.usps.com/

How to address an envelope to send your letter: Google it, or visit the United States Postal Service website.
https://www.usps.com/ship/letters.htm

Julie Merrick's TEDx Camarillo Talk about handwritten letters (You can hear what I've felt for years!)
https://tinyurl.com/julietedxtalk

Subscription Boxes

These companies will send you a variety of cards and more each month. Some include stamps, pens, and other items to ensure you will have everything you need, delivered to your mailbox. A fun and thoughtful gift to send to others, too!

Nicely Noted	Sky of Blue Cards
One-Per-Week	Snail Box Cards
Pretty Paper Club	The Lost Art Stationery

Letter Writing Organizations

From The Heart

Send cards to seniors from around the United States. This is a Facebook Group that lists letter requests and has a birthday list where you can write to someone any day of the year.

Girls Love Mail

Your handwritten letter is sent to women newly diagnosed with breast cancer.

International Pen Friends

Established in 1967 with over 300,000 members, this survey is detailed with questions to match you with your best pen pal.

League of Extraordinary Pen Pals

For letter writing enthusiasts! Take a look at their logo and "About Us" page to see what the group is all about!

More Love Letters

The World Needs More Love Letters is a global love letter writing organization that uses the power behind social media to encourage others to handwrite and mail letters to strangers around the world.

Post Crossings

A project that allows you to send postcards and receive postcards back from random people around the world.

Student Letter Exchange

For over 80 years, they have matched English-speaking pen pals with students ages 9-20 across the U.S. and around the world.

The Letter Project

Its mission is to encourage and empower girls around the world through handwritten letters.

Write On Campaign

Be sure to join the National Letter Writing Campaign every April. This website has brilliant ideas on who and what to write in your letters.

Stationers — for the best greeting cards, stationery, and more!

Alice Louise Press

Bloomwolf Studios

Chez Gagné

Constellation Co.

Dear Beni

Effie's Paper

Egg Press

Elum Designs

Hammerpress

Hello! Lucky

Hello Paper Press

Ink Meets Paper

Jaymes Paper

Karin Gable Calligraphy

Kiss and Punch

Knot and Bow

Lou Paper

Lucky Horse Press

Lumia Designs

Moglea

Oblation Papers and Press

Oddball Press

Of Note Stationers

One-Per-Week

Paisley Paper Co.

Queenie's Cards

Rock Paper Scissors

Row House 14

Sent-Well

Shindig Paperie

Shop Amy Zhang

Slightly Stationery

Smudge Ink

Sugar Cube Press

The Good Days Print Co.

Thimble Press

Tiramisu Paperie

Unblushing

Wild Ink Press

Wishbone Letterpress

YeaOhGreetings

Xolp

Letter Writing-Related Books

A Modern Guide to Thank You Notes by Heidi Bender

How the Post Office Created America by Winifred Gallagher

If You Find This Letter by Hannah Brencher

I Want To Thank You by Gina Hamady

Letters of Note: An Eclectic Collection of Correspondence Deserving of a Wider Audience by Shaun Usher

The Art of the Handwritten Note: A guide for writing heartfelt notes for every occasion by Margaret Shepherd

The Simple Act of Gratitude: How learning to say thank you changed my life by John Kralik

The Thank You Project by Nancy Davis Koh

To the Letter: A Celebration of the Lost Art of Letter Writing by Simon Garfield

Words To The Rescue: The sentiment guide for the tongue-tied by Steve Fadie

Write Back Soon! Adventures in Letter Writing by Karen Benke

A letter for you

Dear Reader,

Thank you for taking the time to write 52 handwritten letters! I hope it was a rewarding experience.

I've always loved the Maya Angelou quote: "I've learned that people will forget what you said, people will forget what you did, but people will never forget how you made them feel." I hope you felt love, joy, gratitude, and much more while writing and sending your letters.

And perhaps you've heard back from some of the people you wrote. I'm sure they were grateful to receive your letters.

In this ever-changing, fast-paced world, we need to let others know they are worthy, loved, and appreciated. You have done that by staying committed to writing to others.

Drop me a letter and let me know the ways you used this journal, what you enjoyed or didn't like, and what you'd like to see in a future edition. You can also follow me on Instagram at @aletteraweek. Be sure to tag #aletteraweek as you continue writing and sending letters.

You completed a yearlong challenge! Let's continue to keep handwritten letters alive!

Love,

Julie

My thank you letter

When you have had an idea in your head for more than five years, there are a lot of people to thank:

Alexandra Franzen, Lindsey Smith, Kayla Floyd, Tracie Kendziora, Woz Flint, and everyone from the Get It Done team.

All of my relatives who wrote to me when I was younger and are now guiding me from above. Thank you for the cards and letters I have kept and cherished for decades.

Bob Merrick. My biggest supporter for 25 years. I love our little life with Champ.

Family: *Mom, Dad, Laurie, Miriam, Kristin, Katie, and aunt Kim.* Always grateful for you!

Fourplay Jazz Quartet for your music, specifically, "Live in Tokyo 2013" on YouTube, that I listen to over and over and over while reading, writing letters or in journals, and on the computer.

Inspirational and invaluable authors and friends: *Allison Garcia, Angela Foley, Dallas Woodburn, Dawn Mena, Felicia Fortosis, George Raveling, Grace Tsuyuki, Hannah Brencher, Hope Miller, Jayne Tillema, Katie Damon, Kelli George, Kent Dobson, Mary Plousha, Matthew Brensilver, Megan Cowan, Michael Gervais, Rob Bell, Ryan Holiday, Steven Pressfield, Susie Maga, and Suzanne Marble.*

Kanoe Namahoe, my editor extraordinaire, and *Julia Lee*, for your amazing eagle-eye proofreading. Thank you both for believing in this project. We have come a long way since Ventura High School.

Kristin Rosemond, thank you for your support and listening to me discuss this project while you were driving to work meetings, on Zoom calls, or walking Beja! SKS!

Millennials, you are the number one age group who are purchasing greeting cards. We need you to keep writing handwritten letters!

My "Soul Sisters", with whom I've been meditating with for a decade now, thank you for allowing me to sit in stillness with you weekly.

United States Postal Workers and mail carriers all over the world, without you, we wouldn't be mailing letters.

Lastly, to all my friends who enjoy corresponding with me through letters throughout the years, and some for decades! Too many to list. Thank you. Thank you. Thank you!

About Julie Merrick

Julie Merrick is a former college athlete, science educator, pilot, mental game coach, and currently teaches mindfulness to students and athletes. She spoke at the TEDx Camarillo event in 2017, about the power of a handwritten letter because she believes mailing letters lets people know they matter.

She loves tacos, reading, stationery, meditating, and orca whales—not necessarily in that order.

This is her first journal, though probably not her last.

Find more about Julie at www.aletteraweek.com.